Rattlesnakes

by Mary Ann McDonald

Illustrated with photographs
by Joe McDonald

Capstone Press

MINNEAPOLIS

Printed in the United States of America.

Capstone Press • 2440 Fernbrook Lane • Minneapolis, MN 55447

Editorial Director   John Coughlan
Managing Editor   Tom Streissguth
Production Editor   Jim Stapleton
Book Designer   Timothy Halldin

Library of Congress Cataloging-in-Publication Data
McDonald, Mary Ann.
   Rattlesnakes / by Mary Ann and Joe McDonald; illustrated with photographs by the authors.
      p. cm.
   Includes bibliographical references (p. 46) and index.
   Summary: Describes the physical characteristics, behavior, and different varieties of rattlesnakes.
   ISBN 1-56065-294-2
   1. Rattlesnakes--Juvenile literature. [1. Rattlesnakes. 2. Snakes.] I. McDonald, Joe. II. Title
   QL666.O69M34 1996
   597.96--dc20   95-436
                                                          CIP
                                                          AC
00 99 98 97 96   8 7 6 5 4 3 2 1

Table of Contents

Fast Facts about Rattlesnakes..............................4

Chapter 1 About the Rattlesnake 7

Chapter 2 Size, Color, and Shape.....................11

Chapter 3 Movement..19

Chapter 4 The Senses......................................25

Chapter 5 Hunting and Defense......................31

Chapter 6 Mating and Reproduction................37

Chapter 7 Rattlesnakes and Humans................41

Glossary...45

To Learn More...47

Some Useful Addresses....................................47

Index...48

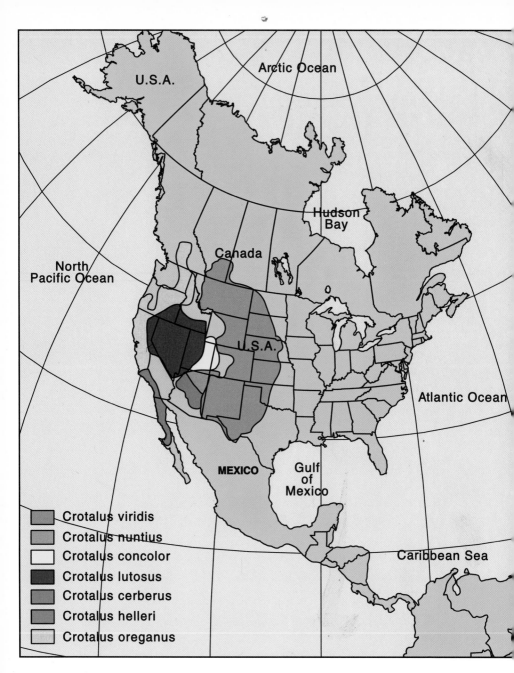

**Seven major species of rattlesnakes inhabit the
United States, Canada, and Mexico.**

Fast Facts about Rattlesnakes

Scientific names: Rattlesnakes are members of the Viperid, or pit viper, family. They are the only snakes to have rattles on their tails.

Description: Rattlesnakes range in length from two to eight feet (0.6 to 2.44 meters). They have many different colors and patterns. These patterns help the snakes to camouflage, or hide, themselves.

Distinctive habits: Rattlesnakes use their **venom** to kill prey, the animals they want to eat.

Food: Rodents, birds, and many kinds of small mammals.

Reproduction: Rattlesnakes give birth to live young. The average number of young varies among species. It is generally between six and 20.

Range: Rattlesnakes range from southern Canada to South America.

Habitat: They live in many different kinds of terrain, including mountains and deserts.

Chapter 1

About the Rattlesnake

During the Revolutionary War, the people of the American colonies added the rattlesnake to their flag as a warning to the British. The rattlesnake showed thirteen rattles, for the thirteen colonies. The rattlesnake, and not the eagle, almost became the national symbol of the United States.

There are at least 30 different rattlesnake species. They live in southern Canada, in most of the United States, in Central America, and in eastern South America. You can find them in

The black-tailed rattlesnake lives in the deserts of southern Arizona.

Rattlesnakes, including this banded rock rattler, use their color patterns as camouflage.

mountainous areas, swamps, grasslands, and deserts.

Some rattlesnakes are found only in certain areas. The sidewinder lives in the deserts of the southwestern United States. Arizona, a southwestern state, has more species of rattlesnake than any other state.

Sleeping in Winter

During the winter, rattlesnakes that live in cold areas **hibernate**, or sleep, in their dens.

These dens can be crevices in rock faces, holes in the ground under trees, or the burrows of other animals. Den openings usually face south, the direction of the winter sun. The dens are deep enough to keep the snakes from freezing during the winter.

Different species of rattlesnakes sometimes share the same den. They also share dens with copperheads, black racers, rat snakes, hognose snakes, and other species of snakes. As many as several hundred snakes may hibernate together.

Dens are important places for rattlesnakes. Many rattlers use the same den all their lives. They mate and give birth nearby. They must always find a den before winter begins. If a snake is unable to hibernate, it will die.

Chapter 2
Size, Color, and Shape

There are two groups of rattlesnakes. The Crotalus group includes the larger snakes like the eastern diamondback. This rattler can reach a length of eight feet (2.4 meters) and weigh up to 20 pounds (nine kilograms). Crotalus rattlesnakes have small scales on their heads. These scales are not much different than their body scales.

Pygmy rattlesnakes and massasaugas are members of the Sistrurus group. Like non-**venomous** snakes, these snakes have nine large

Rattlesnakes gain a new rattle each time they shed their skin.

scales on the tops of their heads. Sistrurus rattlers are small—around two feet (61 centimeters) long. They live in swampy areas. ("Massasauga" is an Indian word meaning "swampy".)

Rattlesnakes have thousands of scales of different sizes. The scales on their backs and sides have ridges, or **keels**, down the middle. Their belly scales are smooth and much larger.

Snake Skin

A rattlesnake has three layers of skin. The bottom layer, which holds the snake's color, is very thick. The scales are part of the thick, middle layer. The bottom and middle layers help protect the snake as it travels over rough surfaces.

The third layer of skin is very thin. It is thin enough to cover the eyes and still allow the snake to see. The rattlesnake sheds this layer of skin as it grows.

Each of the scales on a rattler's skin has a center ridge known as a keel.

Before shedding, the skin over the eye becomes cloudy and bluish. A few days after the eye clears, the rattlesnake begins rubbing its head against something hard. It breaks the old skin, then crawls out of the skin by turning it inside out. The new skin is very shiny and colorful.

Rattles

Rattlesnake rattles are made of **keratin**, the same material that makes up our fingernails

An eastern diamondback rattlesnake slowly sheds an old layer of skin.

A diamondback rattler prepares to strike.

and hair. The rattles make a loud buzzing noise whenever the snake shakes its tail. Some of the larger rattlesnakes can be heard up to 60 feet (18 meters) away.

A rattlesnake grows during its entire lifetime. Depending on how well it eats, and how fast it grows, a rattler may shed several

This pygmy rattlesnake is native to South Carolina and the eastern United States.

times in one year. Everytime the snake sheds, it adds a new rattle. So you can't tell the age of a rattlesnake from the number of its rattles. The largest number of rattles ever recorded on a wild snake is 16.

Inside a Snake

Many people think a snake is all tail. This is not true. The tail is only a small part of the snake's body. Since the body is long and slender, all of the snake's organs are long and slender as well.

Rattlesnakes have the same kinds of organs as humans. A snake has a heart, a stomach, intestines, and usually just one long lung. Snakes also have backbones with many ribs. The more ribs in their backbones, the stronger and more flexible they are. The bones help the snake coil and move in different ways.

Chapter 3

Movement

Have you ever tried to move like a snake? Try lying on the floor and moving in a straight line without using your arms or legs. It can be pretty hard. Rattlesnakes have no arms or legs to help them move. But their bodies have adapted. They can crawl over any surface, climb trees, and even swim.

For the rattlesnake, there are four different ways to move. The way it uses depends on its size, where it lives, and where it wants to go.

Snakes can bend and curl to pass under logs and between narrow ledges of rock.

19

A timber rattlesnake explores rough terrain using serpentine motion.

Moving Like a Snake

The most common type of snake movement is **serpentine motion**. In this motion, the rattlesnake uses its scales to push off of rough surfaces with its belly and sides. The body and tail follow whatever path the head takes. Rattlesnakes also use this motion when swimming.

Larger rattlesnakes use their **scutes**, or scales, for **caterpillar motion**. The snake raises and lowers its scutes to pull itself forward. A person rowing a boat uses the same motion when he or she dips the oars in the water, pulls them back, then raises them and starts over. By using a rippling action of the muscles, the snake puts many scutes into the ground at once. The ripples pull its body forward.

Another common snake movement is **concertina motion**. This method is useful in slippery or confined areas. The snake anchors its tail and reaches forward with the upper part of its body. When it finds a rough surface to hold on to, it will anchor this part and pull its tail up to meet the front. The whole process is then repeated. This looks a little like a person playing a concertina, a kind of accordion.

The last type of motion is handy for snakes living in sandy desert areas. It is called **sidewinding**, and is often used by the sidewinder rattlesnake. With this motion, the

Sidewinders leave telltale tracks in the sand and gravel of desert terrain.

rattlesnake throws its body in loops across the sand. While sidewinding, the rattler looks like a corkscrew rolling across the sand.

The sidewinder moves sideways to the direction that its head is pointing. The snake

first plants its neck in the sand and then loops
its body toward this spot. As it moves, it leaves
a unusual trail shaped like a series of J's. The
rattlesnake makes two J's at a time with the
front part, then makes a new J as the back part
follows.

Chapter 4
The Senses

A rattlesnake is an **ectotherm**, meaning a cold-blooded animal. It can't shiver to get warm or pant to cool off. To warm itself, the snake must lie in the sun. When it gets too warm, it crawls into the shade. Because rattlesnakes are active during the hot summer, most have become nocturnal (active at night) to escape the heat.

How a Rattlesnake Sees

Rattlesnakes have adapted their senses to nocturnal habits. Their eyes have narrow, vertical slits for pupils. These slits open wide at night to help the snake see better. A rattlesnake has no eyelids, so it can't close its eyes. Even when they are sleeping, rattlers look wide awake.

Snakes have very poor eyesight. They can see only as far as about 15 inches (38 centimeters) in front of them. If it can't see its prey clearly, a rattlesnake will react to movement. This can get the snake in trouble if

The ridges above a sidewinder's eyes protect them from the blowing sand.

it strikes at a cow, a human, or another large animal.

Some snakes that live in the desert have ridges above their eyes. These ridges help the snake to see. While waiting for prey, a sidewinder will bury itself in the sand with only its eyes showing above the sand. The ridges act like a fence. They keep the blowing sand from covering the eyes. The sidewinder's ridges have earned this snake the nickname of horned rattler.

A Sensitive Snake

Rattlesnakes can't hear sounds, but they can sense vibrations. Like other snakes, they have internal ears instead of external ones. When a snake lays its head on the ground, it picks up vibrations with its jawbones. The vibrations travel to the internal ears. This allows the rattlesnake to feel the vibrations of animals or people long before they can see them.

Rattlesnakes are deaf, so they can't hear themselves rattle. They use their rattles to warn large mammals, such as bison or deer, that they

Snakes use their forked tongues to test the air for the scent of prey.

are too close. The rattling tail is probably a nervous reaction to danger, since many other species of snakes also use this warning.

Smell and Taste

Rattlesnakes smell in two ways. They have nostrils and can smell like people do. But they can also use their tongue to smell.

A rattlesnake often flicks its long, forked tongue in and out of its mouth. Every time the tongue is out, the snake picks up small dust particles from the air and ground. Inside the mouth, the tongue rubs against special taste detectors called Jacobson's organs. Rattlesnakes use their tongues and Jacobson's organs to follow scent trails, find prey, and recognize other snakes.

Rattlesnakes also have two heat-sensing pits. These are openings between the nose and eyes that help them locate prey. The snake moves its head slowly back and forth, using its pits to sense where the strongest heat is coming from. The pits sense the heat of warm-blooded animals from a long distance. Even in total darkness, a rattlesnake can be very accurate when it strikes.

Chapter 5
Hunting and Defense

Rattlesnakes are venomous. Their bite contains venom, or poison, that helps the snake catch its prey. The venom not only kills the prey, but it also starts the digestive process.

There are two types of rattlesnake venom. **Hemotoxins** attack the blood cells and the tissues of the prey, causing bruising and internal bleeding. **Neurotoxins** affect the nerves of the prey, especially those that help breathing and the heart. Most rattlesnakes have

Rattles are used to warn approaching enemies. Most animals will carefully heed this warning.

more hemotoxins than neurotoxins, but all have both.

Fangs

Rattlesnakes have special hollow teeth, called **fangs**, in the front of their mouths. Normally the fangs fold back into the mouth and only come forward when the snake strikes. Some rattlesnakes have more than one pair of fangs. If one pair breaks off, a set of new fangs replaces them.

Long, hollow tubes connect the fangs with poison sacs at the back of the rattlesnake's head. These sacs give the snake's head its triangular shape. When the rattlesnake bites its prey, strong muscles squirt the venom through the fangs and into the prey.

A Rattlesnake Ambush

Along a forest path, a rattlesnake lies motionless. The snake waits patiently for hours. Suddenly, a small animal appears. The rattlesnake strikes like lightning. The victim doesn't even know what hit it.

A timber rattlesnake bares its fangs.

Most of the time, the rattlesnake will let go after biting its victim. The animal won't run far, because the venom acts fast. The rattlesnake waits a few minutes, then uses its tongue to follow the prey's scent. Once it finds the victim, it will search for the head. Rattlesnakes eat most of their food head first.

Squirrels or rats with large teeth can injure the rattlesnake in a fight. The venom allows the snake to strike, let go, and eat a few minutes later in safety. If a rattlesnake bites a bird or lizard, it will hold on. Otherwise, the animal might fly or leap too far away, and the rattlesnake may not find its meal.

Rattlesnakes eat many types of prey—everything from frogs and earthworms to lizards and rabbits. Rodents, such as mice and rats, are their favorites.

The rattlesnake uses its poisonous venom to stun its prey, then eats slowly as the helpless victim dies.

A rattlesnake can eat prey that is much larger than its head. When it eats something large, its jaws come apart, allowing its mouth to open wide. The rattlesnake has no teeth and swallows its meal whole. When it has finished, the rattlesnake yawns and puts its jaws back in place.

Rattlesnakes have many enemies. Hawks and owls hunt and eat rattlesnakes. In the desert, roadrunners, foxes, and coyotes prey on the sidewinder. Bison and other large mammals trample snakes that cross their path. Other snakes are also a danger. The indigo snake, an endangered species in the southeastern United States, eats rattlesnakes it finds in its burrow.

Chapter 6

Mating and Reproduction

Mating occurs in the spring, after the rattlesnake crawls out of its den. If there are no males around, the female leaves a scent trail for them to follow. If several males show up at once, there may be a showdown.

Male rattlesnakes perform a special dance to decide which will mate with the female. Two males face each other and raise the front part of their bodies high. They push and shove each other, but they never bite. The stronger one wins by pushing the other down. The winner then mates with the female.

Courtship and Mating

Like birds, rattlesnakes go through a courtship. The male rubs his chin along the body of the female, then the two snakes wrap their tails around each other. The female is usually larger and stronger. If she moves, she'll drag the male along with her.

After mating, the male leaves for its summer feeding grounds. The female stays at the den site until she gives birth. Rattlesnakes **drop** their young in late summer. The female may not eat at all before giving birth. If she doesn't eat enough before going into hibernation, she will probably die during the winter.

Young Snakes

Rattlesnakes give birth to between 6 and 20 live young. Before it's born, a young rattlesnake grows inside the mother in its own egg sac. It must break out of this clear sac before the birth.

Rattlesnakes are born with a tiny knob, called the **prebutton**, on the end of their tails.

The venomous black-tailed rattlesnake prefers hot climates and desert terrain.

Within two weeks, the baby rattlesnake sheds its skin, and the first rattle appears. This rattle is called the **button**. The button is silent, since two or more rattles must shake against each other to make noise.

Rattlesnake young are born close to the time of hibernation. To help the young survive, the mother leaves a scent trail that leads to the den. Some young snakes hibernate without eating. By spring, they are very hungry.

Chapter 7
Rattlesnakes and Humans

Rattlesnakes have played an important role in the history and culture of Native American tribes. The Hopi Indians of Arizona perform a Snake Dance using live rattlesnakes. The ancient Aztec and Mayan people of Central America worshiped rattlesnakes. One of their most famous gods, Quetzalcoatl, was part rattlesnake.

Many people hate or fear rattlesnakes. In the past, some towns held "rattlesnake round-ups." People caught and killed hundreds of

A young albino diamondback rattlesnake takes cover near a rock.

rattlesnakes. They ate the meat or used the snakes for decorations.

In the south, people poured gasoline and other chemicals into rattlesnake burrows. This drove the rattlesnakes out, but it also killed good animals such as the indigo snake, the gopher frog, and the gopher tortoise. These three animals are now threatened or endangered.

In some areas, the law now protects rattlesnakes. Any captured rattlesnake must be returned at the end of a roundup to the exact spot where it was found. And it is against the law to use chemicals to drive snakes from their burrows.

You can enjoy hikes in rattlesnake country without fear if you follow these steps. Read about the area where you will be hiking and find out what types of snakes live there. Wear leather hiking boots and long, loose pants. Always step onto a log before going over it. Always look before you sit down, and be careful where you place your hands.

Meeting a Rattlesnake

If you see a rattlesnake:
✔ Freeze, then
✔ Walk slowly backwards, facing the snake
✔ Be careful not to step on another snake as you retreat.
✔ Don't kill the rattlesnake and don't try to catch it. Many people have been bitten while trying to cut the rattles from a snake they thought was dead.

Heavy boots and a careful step will help when traveling through rattlesnake country.

If you are bitten:
✔ Don't panic. Sit quietly.
✔ Check if the fangs have broken the skin.
✔ Try to get a good look at the snake from a safe distance.
✔ Have someone else go for help.
✔ If you must move, walk slowly, but get to a doctor as soon as you can.

Despite their bad reputations, rattlesnakes are an important part of our natural world. Their venom has been used to treat many kinds of illness, and they help control rats and mice. They are beautiful snakes—but it's best to enjoy them from a distance.

Glossary

button–the first rattle that a young rattlesnake grows

caterpillar motion–a motion used by snakes, especially larger ones, to move in a straight line

concertina motion–a motion used by snakes in a confined area or when it is slippery

drop–to give birth

ectotherm–a cold-blooded animal. Ectotherms must warm themselves by lying in the sun and cool themselves by hiding under different objects

fangs–hollow teeth that snakes use to inject venom into their prey

hemotoxin–a poison that attacks the blood cells and tissues of an animal

hibernate–to sleep or to be inactive during the cold months of the year

keratin–a dry, non-living material that makes up bone, fingernails, hair, and feathers

keels–ridges that run down the middle of the scales on the back and sides of a rattlesnake

neurotoxin–a poison that affects the nerves used in breathing and in making the heart beat

prebutton–a small knob on a newborn rattlesnake that develops into the snake's first rattle

scute–the large belly scales used in different kinds of motion

serpentine motion–a motion used by snakes to move along rough surfaces. Snakes also use serpentine motion when they swim.

sidewinding–a motion used by snakes in desert or sandy areas

venom–a poisonous saliva in some snakes

venomous–poisonous: an animal or plant containing poison

To Learn More

Freedman, Russel. *Killer Snakes.* New York: Holiday House, 1982.

Gross, Ruth Below. *Snakes.* New York: Four Winds Press, 1990.

Lavies, Bianca. *The Secretive Timber Rattlesnake.* New York: Dutton, 1990.

Simon, Seymour. *Snakes.* New York: Harper Collins, 1992.

Smith, Roland. *Snakes in the Zoo.* Brookfield, CT: Millbrook Press, 1992.

Where to see Rattlesnakes

Sonora Desert Museum, Tucson, Arizona

National Zoo, Washington DC

Clyde Peeling's Reptiland, Williamsport, PA

Toronto Zoo, Toronto, Ontario, Canada

Dallas Zoo, Dallas, Texas

Index

Arizona, 8

camouflage, 5
Canada, 7
caterpillar
 motion, 21
colors, 5
concertina
 motion, 21
Crotalus group,
 11

ears, 27
Eastern
 diamondback,
 11
eyes, 12, 14, 25-
 27

fangs, 32, 44

habitat, 5, 7
hibernation, 8-9,
 38-39

hiking, 43
Hopi Indians, 41

indigo snakes,
 35, 42

Jacobson's
 organs, 29
jawbones, 27, 34

keels, 12
keratin, 14

massasaugas, 11-
 12
mating, 37

pits, 29
poison sacs, 32
prebuttons, 38
pygmy
 rattlesnakes, 11

range, 5

rattles, 4, 7, 14-
 16, 28, 39

scales, 11-12, 20-
 21
serpentine
 motion, 20-21
shedding, 14, 16,
 38-39
sidewinder, 8,
 22-23, 27, 35
Sisturus group,
 11
smell, 29

tails, 17, 20-21
tongues, 29, 33

venom, 5, 31-33,
 44